EVERYDAY LIFE IN ROMAN TIMES

MIKE CORBISHLEY

FRANKLIN WATTS
LONDON · SYDNEY

This edition published in 2003 by
Franklin Watts
96 Leonard Street
London EC2A 4XD

Franklin Watts Australia
45-51 Huntley Street
Alexandria
NSW 2015

ISBN 0 7496 2031 5

A CIP catalogue record for this book is available
from the British Library.

Editor: Sarah Ridley
Designer: Alan Cassedy
Illustrators: Peter Kesteven and Ray Grinaway
Picture researcher: Joanne King

Photographs: Ancient Art and Architecture Collection
7b, 18t, 20t, 25b; courtesy of the Trustees of the British
Museum 7t, 8t, 10t, 22t, 26t; Colchester Museums 24t;
Mike Corbishley 6t; Michael Holford 6c, 16t (both), 28t;
Museum of London 6b; Vindolanda Trust 14t; Roger White 12t;
reproduced by courtesy of the Yorkshire
Museum/Woodmansterne 5t, 30t.

Printed in Dubai, UAE

CONTENTS

WHO WERE THE ROMANS?

Two thousand years ago, the Romans were the most powerful nation in Europe and around the Mediterranean Sea. About 60 million people lived in the countries which made up their empire. The official language of all these people was Latin but they spoke their own languages as well – languages such as ancient Greek and Celtic.

Their empire began when the tribe known as the *Latins* took over the city of Rome in Italy and began to conquer the lands all around them. They became known as the Romans. Wherever they went they built towns and introduced Roman life, including the Latin language, to new peoples. You will find Latin words in several modern languages. Also, many towns in Europe were originally founded by the Romans.

Roman coins

This is a map (right) of what the Roman world looked like about 1800 years ago. All these lands became part of the Roman Empire when they were conquered by the Roman army. Each new land (such as *Britannia* or *Arabia*) was known as a *province* of the Empire. Towards the end of the Roman period, this Empire was divided in two. The west was ruled from Rome and the east from Constantinople (now Istanbul in Turkey).

BRITANNIA

BELGICA

LUGDUNENSIS
GALLIA

AQUITANIA

ATLANTIC OCEAN

NARBONENS

TARRACONENSIS

LUSITANIA

BAETICA

MAURETANIA
CEASARIENSIS

MAURETANIA
TINGITANA

SOME IMPORTANT DATES FROM ROMAN TIMES

BC 800-400

753 Legend says Rome was founded by Romulus.

509 Latins throw Etruscans out of Rome. Roman state established.

BC 400-100

264-241, 237-202, 149-146 Rome at war with the Carthaginians.
218 Carthaginian general Hannibal crosses Alps with elephants to invade Italy.
146 Rome conquers North Africa and Greece.

BC 100-0

44 Julius Caesar becomes Roman Dictator after several civil wars.
59-49 Caesar conquers Gaul and invades Britain.
27 Augustus becomes Rome's first emperor.

AD 0-100

14 Emperor Augustus dies.
29 Jesus Christ crucified.
43 Emperor Claudius conquers Britain.
79 Vesuvius erupts – Pompeii and Herculaneum destroyed.

WHAT DID THE ROMANS LOOK LIKE?

Some portraits of Roman people have survived. They show that you can't describe a typical Roman as the people looked different all round the Empire.

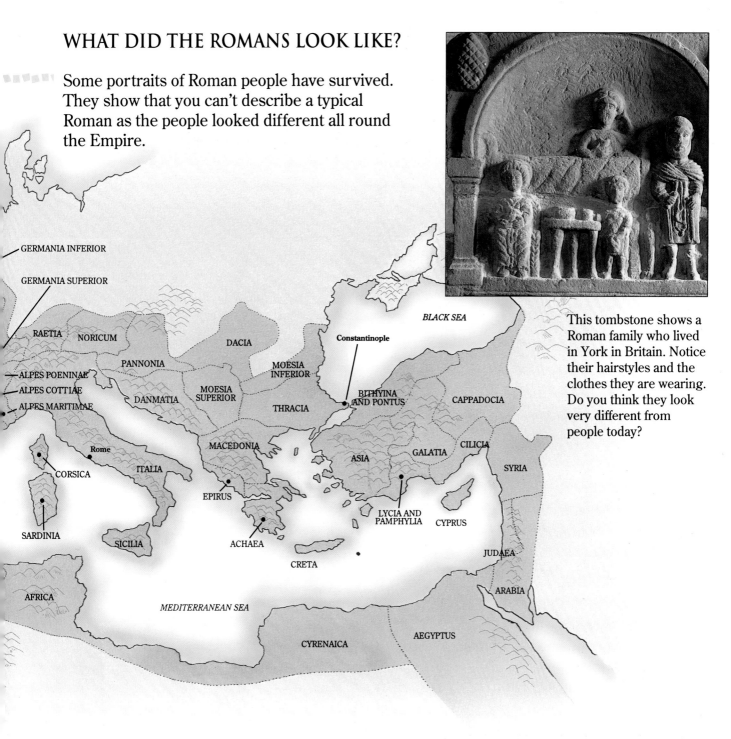

This tombstone shows a Roman family who lived in York in Britain. Notice their hairstyles and the clothes they are wearing. Do you think they look very different from people today?

AD 100-200

114 Emperor Trajan builds huge column in Rome to celebrate victories in war.
122 Hadrian's Wall begun in Britain.

AD 200-300

212 All men (not women) in the *provinces* are made Roman citizens.
267 Athens captured by Goths.
284 Empire divided and ruled from two capitals.

AD 300-400

312 Constantine is Rome's first Christian emperor.
330 Emperor Constantine moves his capital and founds Constantinople.
367 Britain attacked by 'barbarians'.

AD 400-600

409 Vandal armies begin to invade Europe.
476 German armies throw out last emperor in Rome.
540 Roman armies from Constantinople reconquer Italy.

Detectives look for clues to help them solve crimes. Archaeologists and historians looking at the past call their clues evidence. We can find out about the Romans through three sorts of evidence – Roman writing, standing buildings and the clues discovered by archaeologists.

Excavating a Roman site is a fiddly business. Here archaeologists are carefully removing layers of earth, making a record of everything they find.

ARCHAEOLOGICAL EVIDENCE

What do you think happens to the things you throw away? When your dustbin has been emptied, some things, such as paper and food remains, rot quite quickly. Other materials take longer to rot, like fabric and wood, and some will take years to rot, or won't rot at all, like metals and glass.

In the same way, only some objects from Roman times survive today. Many of these objects have been found in Roman rubbish pits (their dustbins!), Roman sites or sometimes in Roman graves. Archaeologists have to decide what all this evidence means and what it tells them about life in Roman times. We often have more objects from rich people than poor people, for example.

Colourful mosaics on the floors of Roman houses give us all sorts of clues about everyday life. Here is the grape harvest being brought in for pressing into wine.

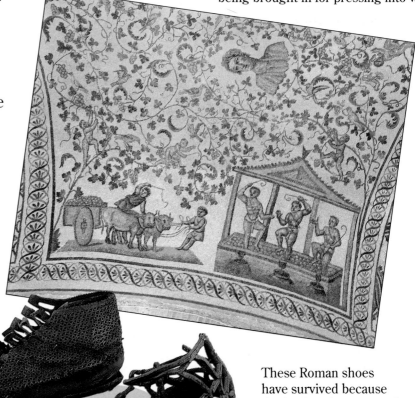

These Roman shoes have survived because the leather they are made from was preserved in wet ground.

ROMAN WRITING

The Romans left us a lot of their writing – histories of their empire, plays, poems, recipe books and letters, for example. Very rarely do the original pieces of writing survive. However, we can still read today what the Romans wrote because many of their books were copied out by monks in the medieval period.

One letter that has survived was found at the site of Vindolanda, one of the forts of Hadrian's Wall, the Roman frontier in Britain. The letter was written in ink on a very thin piece of wood (see page 20 for more about writing). It is a party invitation asking Lepidinia to Claudia Severa's birthday party on 3rd September.

STANDING STRUCTURES

In some places, we don't have to search to find out what it was like in Roman times. Many Roman buildings have survived, especially in North Africa and in the eastern part of the Mediterranean. Sometimes the remains of whole towns survive, such as Pompeii which was buried under volcanic ash in 79.

This amphitheatre, called the Colosseum, was built for gladiators to fight in as entertainment for the people of Rome (see pages 24-25). A lot of the building has survived for two thousand years.

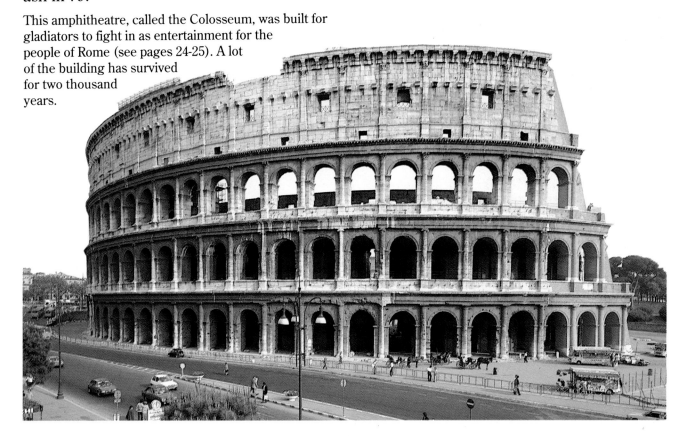

ON THE FARM

Have you ever seen anything like this before? It's a difficult question because one part is missing – the handle. It has rotted away but the rusty iron blade of this sickle has survived.

Farmworkers used sickles like this to cut crops in the fields. They grabbed a handful of corn with one hand and cut through the tough stalks with the sickle.

The edge would have been kept very sharp with a sharpening stone called a whetstone.

FARMING

The Romans did not use machinery to farm as we usually do today. There were ploughs, of course, and a range of special farm tools but the most important 'tool' a farmer had was the workforce. This was largely made up of slaves in the Roman world, people taken prisoner in the wars across the Empire.

Huge numbers of people had to be fed and bread was the staple food for many of them. The very poor people living in the capital city of Rome relied on free hand-outs of bread from the government. Most of the wheat needed for all that bread came from the Roman *province* of Egypt.

Not all farms in the Roman world were large estates worked by slave labour. There were many small farms, especially in Italy, worked by a family with only one or two slaves.

MYSTERY
O B J E C T

If you lived in Roman times you might have seen this clever piece of equipment on a farm. Can you guess what it was? You will find the answer on page 32.

Farm workers cut the
barley with sickles in
small fields near the *villa*.

SOME OF THE CROPS GROWN BY THE ROMANS

Radishes

Cabbages

Lettuces

Carrots

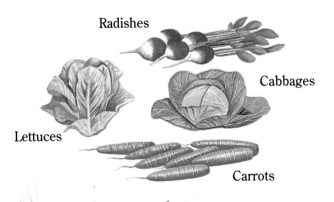

Oats

Barley

Dates

Apples

Pears

Cherries

Grapes

ON THE ROMAN VILLA

A big farming estate was called a *villa* –
the word the Romans also used for a
farmhouse or a country or seaside house.
Rich Romans often had a number of *villas* in
different parts of a *province*, or in Italy itself.
A farm might specialise in one crop or be
'mixed', like the one pictured above.

When the owner wasn't on the farm, the
work was supervised by a farm manager
who usually had his own house. Nearby
would have been a dormitory for the farm
slaves as well as barns for animals, crops
and equipment.

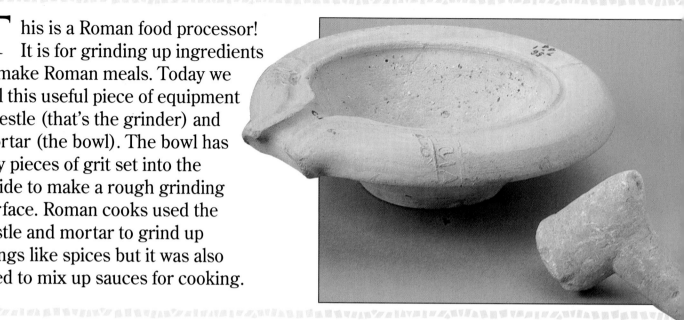

This is a Roman food processor! It is for grinding up ingredients to make Roman meals. Today we call this useful piece of equipment a pestle (that's the grinder) and mortar (the bowl). The bowl has tiny pieces of grit set into the inside to make a rough grinding surface. Roman cooks used the pestle and mortar to grind up things like spices but it was also used to mix up sauces for cooking.

EATING OUT

Only wealthy Roman families had proper kitchens to prepare their meals. Everyone else either ate out, or cooked over a basic grill *brazier* in their flat. This created a high fire risk in many Roman flats which were wood-built. So, various emperors made it illegal to cook at home, forcing people to eat out.

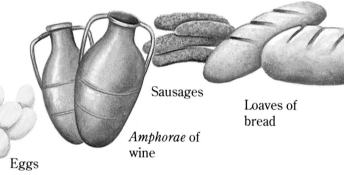

Sausages

Loaves of bread

Amphorae of wine

Eggs

Olives

There were lots of different foods on offer for people walking through the town.

Bars, like the one shown (*left*) from the Roman port of Ostia in Italy, sold a variety of snacks and drinks. Wall paintings showed the customers what was on offer – eggs, turnips and green olives, for example. You might have a glass of honey water to drink or hot spiced wine. There were tables and benches inside or you could just eat and drink at the bar.

Slaves did the cooking in the Roman kitchen. They would be kept busy preparing meals and banquets for their master and mistress.

MAKE YOUR OWN
SWEETS

You can make real Roman sweets at home. Here are two recipes from the Roman cookery writer called Apicius.

STUFFED DATES:

Take the stones out of the dates. Now fill the insides with nuts or pine kernels or ground pepper. Roll the dates in salt and fry them in warmed honey.

HONEYED BREAD:

Remove the crusts from a wholemeal loaf and break into pieces (not too small). Soak the pieces in milk then fry in olive oil. Pour over some honey before serving.

IN THE KITCHEN

Romans ate their food highly spiced with lots of different ingredients. Roman cooks made their own sauces but they also bought one called *liquamen* which was made from salted fish and fish insides.

Cooking was done in ovens or over a little fire on the surface. An iron grid held the metal pans over the hot charcoal. Vegetables and herbs were hung up to dry. There were always some very large pottery containers for storing flour, wine, *liquamen* or dried vegetables.

This is a couch from the Roman town of Herculaneum. Only the wooden frame survives now but originally it would have been upholstered; stuffing covered with coloured material would have been used to make it soft. Cushions, stuffed with wool, feathers or straw, would have made this a very comfortable piece of furniture.

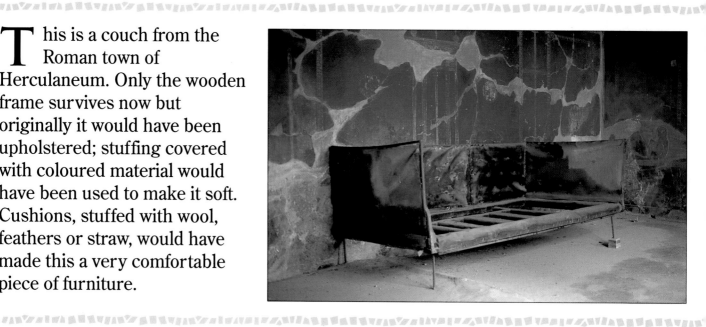

TYPES OF HOUSES

If you could afford it you would live, with your family and slaves, in a private house with rooms set around an inner courtyard open to the sky. There would be more rooms at the back of the house around a garden.

But many people lived in blocks of flats in towns and rented a single room or an apartment. In Rome these blocks of flats were five or six storeys high but elsewhere they were usually only two or three storeys high.

IN THE GARDEN

Rich peoples' houses had gardens surrounded by a covered walk which shaded people from the sun. The garden was usually laid out very carefully with hedges of the box plant. You would see herbs and fruit trees there, as well as flowers. Many gardens had fountains and water basins. Statues were popular in gardens too and some statues even had their own fountains built in.

Grapevines

Fennel

Mint

Parsley

Bay tree

Fig tree

Apple tree

Cherry tree

The mistress of the house in one of the 'living' rooms. Notice the low table and cupboard – like our furniture today.

Mosaic from a living room floor at Lullingstone Roman *villa*, England.

WALLS AND FLOORS

The Romans liked their houses to be decorated. They had not invented wallpaper but they did bring in artists to paint pictures on the walls. Owners of houses also hung painted wood panels on their walls. Sometimes the panels were plain but more often they showed a scene.

The favourite type of high quality flooring was the mosaic. This was made from little tiles of different coloured stone or brick. Artists set the thousands of pieces into elaborate patterns or pictures.

Common mosaic patterns

WHAT SHALL I WEAR TODAY?

This is a leather sandal made for a Roman lady who lived in Britain. We even know the name of the shoemaker. He stamped his name on the sole. It reads L. AEB. THALES T.F. which is short for Lucius Aebutius Thales, son of Titus. This sandal was of the highest quality, perhaps to wear on special occasions when guests came to the house. You can see it's very like ones still used today. Do you have a pair of flip-flops like this?

CLOTHES FOR ALL

You can see from the drawings in this book what kinds of clothes Roman people wore. However, very few actual clothes survive as fabric and leather is quick to rot. We know what the Romans wore mostly from statues and paintings.

Men, women and children wore underclothes. The clothes people wore over these showed what sort of people they were. Slaves and working people wore tunics and in some colder parts of the Roman world they even wore trousers.

A Roman lady would wear an under tunic and then a long dress. In cold weather, she would wear a very large shawl to cover her head and body when she went outside.

If a man was a Roman citizen then he could wear the *toga* over his tunic. Children wore simple tunics like those worn by their parents.

SOME ROMAN WORDS FOR CLOTHES

Bracae - skin-tight trousers worn under a tunic
Palla - shawl worn by women over head and shoulders
Petasus - hat with a broad brim to keep off the sun and the rain
Reticulum - hair net
Stola - woman's long dress

HOW TO TIE YOUR TOGA

The *toga* (A) was a semi-circle in shape. Its width was three times the height of the person wearing it. To put it on, the man had to drape one corner over the left shoulder until it reached his foot (B). He passed the other end under his right arm and across his left shoulder (C). It then had to be pinned, tucked and held in place.

The master and mistress are attended by one of the house slaves.

JEWELLERY

If they could afford it, Roman people wore brightly coloured clothes – women more than men. They also wore jewellery. A woman's hair might be held in place with pins – often carved from bone. Several have been found with carved heads of ladies on them.

Earrings were made from metal and precious stones and were very popular. Matching necklaces were common too, just as they are today. Men and women needed brooches and decorated pins to hold their loose-fitting clothes together. Rings were often worn.

HAIRSTYLES

Women's hairstyles could be simple or very elaborate. Some women dyed their hair or wore wigs made from real hair. Men might go to the hairdresser too, to get their hair curled as well as cut.

KEEPING CLEAN

I magine life without soap! The Romans hadn't discovered soap so they found other ways of getting rid of the dirt. In the bathhouse, warm oil mixed with pumice stone powder was rubbed into the skin. The body would sweat in the heat and the steam. Sweat, dirt and oil would then be scraped off with this instrument, called a *strigil*. It was usually slaves who performed this work.

Strigil

Oil flask

IN THE BATHHOUSE

All Roman towns had at least one public bathhouse. A bathhouse was cheap to enter and free for children. But it was not at all like having a bath today, or even going to a modern swimming baths.

First you undressed and went into a cold room for a cold dip. From there you went to a warm room and then into the really hot steamy room and a hot dip. Sometime later, after a slave had massaged oil into your skin and scraped it off with a *strigil,* you went back to the cold room for a cold dip. You might even take some exercise outside.

1. Undressing room
2. Hot steamy room with hot bath
3. Cold dip bath
4. Exercise yard
5. Open pool

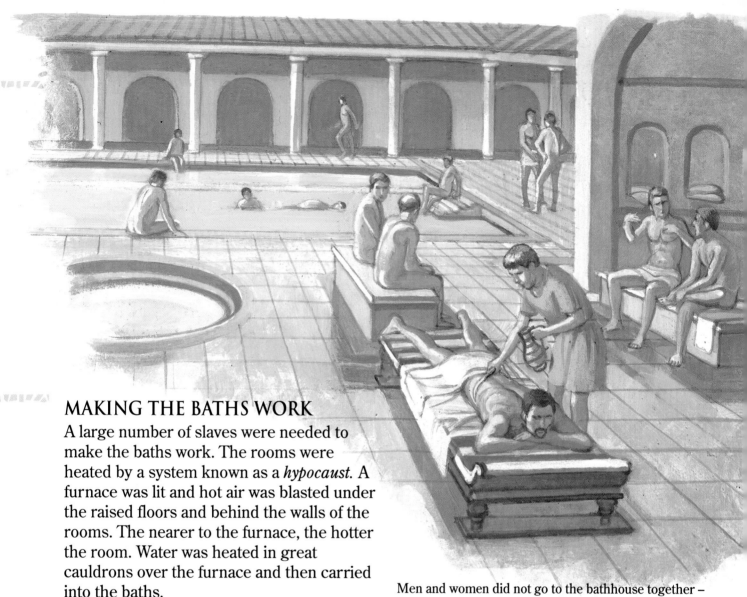

MAKING THE BATHS WORK

A large number of slaves were needed to make the baths work. The rooms were heated by a system known as a *hypocaust*. A furnace was lit and hot air was blasted under the raised floors and behind the walls of the rooms. The nearer to the furnace, the hotter the room. Water was heated in great cauldrons over the furnace and then carried into the baths.

Men and women did not go to the bathhouse together – there were separate sessions. It was a place to go to relax, chat with friends, have a bite to eat or even to conduct some business.

MYSTERY OBJECT

This little object is made of bronze. It is only 6 cm long and could easily be carried on a belt or in a little bag. It would be of great use to anyone wanting to get really clean in the baths.
Can you guess what it was used for?
The answer is on page 32.

RELAXING

One of the favourite activities in the bathhouse was to play games and the Romans also liked to bet. There were games with knucklebones – they were thrown to see which side they landed on. Romans also played dice, either betting on what number would be thrown or using it to play a board game with coloured counters.

This Roman tombstone tells us a lot about life at the time. Waiting for the butcher to prepare her order, this Roman housewife sits in a comfortable chair with her shopping list in front of her. Can you see what the butcher has hung up for sale? He is chopping meat, perhaps chops, on a three-legged block. Some butchers still use these today.

GOING SHOPPING

Shops in Roman towns were open onto the street. In the early morning, the shopkeeper opened up the padlocks which fixed the shutters to the pavement. Some shops had signs advertising their trade – a leg of pork for a butcher's, for example.

Most Roman shops actually produced their goods for sale on the premises. If you went to buy fresh bread, you would see the flour being ground, the dough made and the bread being baked in a great oven.

The Romans used money to buy things, just as we do today. One emperor even fixed the price of all goods and services right across the huge Empire.

All coins had the emperor's head on one side. The coin with the smallest value was the *as,* followed by the *dupondius,* the *sestertius,* the *denarius* and finally the *aureus.*

This was painted on the doorway of the shop of a clothmaker called Verecundus who lived in the city of Pompeii. Under the paintings of gods with elephants, the artist has shown wool being cleaned, woven and then sold at the counter.

Roman streets were always very busy and noisy when the shops were open – in fact several writers complained about the noise and the dirt.

SOME OF THE GOODS AVAILABLE IN A ROMAN SHOPPING STREET

Comb and mirror

Swan to eat

Pillow

Fancy glassware and pottery

THINGS TO BUY

There were no supermarkets in Roman towns so shoppers had to go from one place to another to buy all they needed. Many shopkeepers and craftspeople lived in rooms behind, or on top of, their shops and workshops. Their work often spilled out onto the pavement, as it does in towns in many parts of the world today.

The countryside around the town provided fresh produce to sell in the shops, or more likely in the open-air markets in the town's squares. People also hawked goods in the street, selling goods such as sausages and pease-puddings from trays carried on their head.

This object shows one of the ways the Romans used to write things down. It is a re-usable writing tablet. The wooden frame held a wax surface. The writing was done with the other object shown, called a *stylus*. The sharp end was for scratching the letters onto the surface of the wax. The other flat end was used to rub the words out. When the wax became too thin to write on, more heated wax had to be poured into the wooden frame.

WRITING MATERIALS

Wax tablets were not the only things the Romans wrote on. Thin layers of wood were written on with pen and ink. Books were written on scrolls made of papyrus. Papyrus is a special water plant found mainly in Egypt. The best and most expensive surface the Romans used to write on is called vellum. This is the skin of an animal such as a goat or a lamb which has been made as thin as paper.

You can see Roman numerals in use today. Look for them on watches and clocks. You will also find them on inscriptions cut into stone on public buildings.

THE ROMAN ALPHABET IS SHOWN ABOVE.
TRY USING IT TO WRITE A SENTENCE LIKE THE ONE BELOW.

READ ALL ABOUT THE ROMANS

CAN YOU READ WHAT IT SAYS?

Few girls went to secondary school. Roman fathers usually considered it a waste to educate their daughters.

WRITERS

Homer wrote two long poems in Greek in about 800 BC; the *Iliad* and the *Odyssey*.

Virgil was born in 70 BC and wrote a story poem about the foundation of Rome, called the *Aeneid,* amongst others poems.

Cicero was a Roman politician born in 106 BC. He was famous for his public speeches which were published and used in schools.

Julius Caesar wrote accounts of his own military campaigns against the Gauls which were used in schools as history books.

Seneca wrote an enormous number of books during his lifetime, mainly about the way Romans should conduct their lives.

THE SCHOOL

Boys, and some girls, went to their first school at the age of seven. They learnt the basic subjects of reading, writing and arithmetic from schoolmasters who set up schools in rented rooms or in their own houses. At eleven, pupils went on to a secondary school to be taught by a teacher called a *grammaticus*. They studied the literature of the Greeks (like Homer) and the Romans (like Virgil), history, arithmetic, geometry and astronomy.

| Homer | Virgil | Cicero | Julius Caesar | Seneca |

MAKING JOURNEYS

T he Romans did not have signposts but they did have milestones. This one comes from north Wales. Like other Roman milestones, it gives the number of miles from a place. Can you see KANOVIO M P V111? This means 8 (VIII) miles (M P) from a place called Kanovium. The letters and numbers on the stone would have stood out clearly because they would have been painted with bright colours.

THE NEED FOR ROADS

You can see from the map on pages 4-5 just how big the Roman Empire was. Many people needed to travel as fast as they could across it. The army had to reach trouble spots, merchants needed to carry goods and officials needed to travel to govern the Empire. The Emperor Augustus developed an official courier service to carry both letters and people travelling on public business.

Roads had to be built everywhere. At first this was the army's job as they conquered new lands. After these lands became Roman, it was up to the local government to maintain them and build new ones.

The Romans built their roads as straight as possible, to make travel speedy. The surface was raised above the surrounding land to keep it free from water. Layers of gravel and stone were pounded down to make a hard-wearing surface.

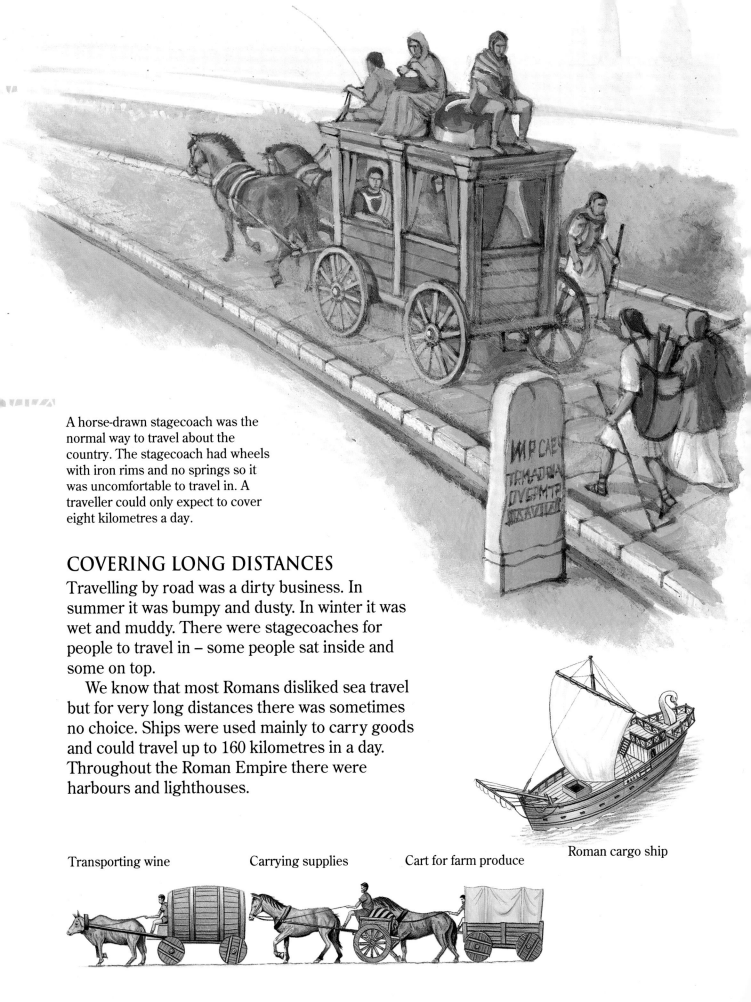

A horse-drawn stagecoach was the normal way to travel about the country. The stagecoach had wheels with iron rims and no springs so it was uncomfortable to travel in. A traveller could only expect to cover eight kilometres a day.

COVERING LONG DISTANCES

Travelling by road was a dirty business. In summer it was bumpy and dusty. In winter it was wet and muddy. There were stagecoaches for people to travel in – some people sat inside and some on top.

We know that most Romans disliked sea travel but for very long distances there was sometimes no choice. Ships were used mainly to carry goods and could travel up to 160 kilometres in a day. Throughout the Roman Empire there were harbours and lighthouses.

Roman cargo ship

Transporting wine   Carrying supplies   Cart for farm produce

GOING TO A SHOW

This is a decorated pot made in the Roman town of Colchester in Britain. All round the pot are scenes of gladiators fighting. These two have their names written above them. Memnon (on the left) is heavily armed and has armour on. He has just beaten Valentinus who is armed with a three-pronged spear (on the ground). He holds up one finger to ask for mercy.

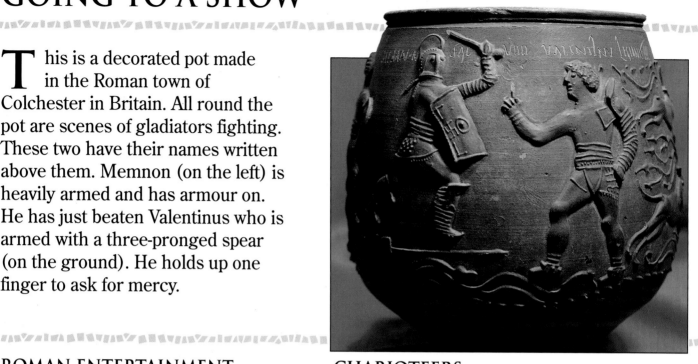

ROMAN ENTERTAINMENT

Romans who lived in towns had a variety of shows to go to as well as the fights between gladiators. There were also theatres and chariot races. Special buildings were put up for these sports and entertainment. Thousands attended, perhaps 20,000 to a play at the theatre, 50,000 to watch the gladiators and 200,000 at the chariot races.

CHARIOTEERS

Charioteers drove chariots pulled by four horses and competed in four separate teams. They wore the team's colours – the Reds, the Blues, the Greens and the Whites. The teams had to complete seven laps in all. Romans loved to bet on the races and charioteers could become millionaires.

Gladiators usually fought to the death. The crowd loved to watch these horrible fights but sometimes spared a loser's life.

Actors preparing for a performance.

MUSIC AND THEATRE

There were plenty of opportunities for Romans to watch plays and listen to music in the theatre. They liked Greek plays, both serious ones and comedies, but there were Roman writers of plays, too. Actors wore face masks to help throw their voices in the huge theatres. The type of mask and the costume worn helped the audience understand the story. For example, actors wore red wigs to play slaves and purple clothes to play young men. Music was usually performed as part of theatre plays but concerts were given as well, often in a little theatre called an *odeon*.

IN THE ARMY

Roman soldiers wore specially designed helmets. This one is made of iron with bronze decoration. Apart from the head protection, there would have been a neck guard and cheek pieces. This helmet was used by a soldier who fought on horseback, a cavalryman. The helmets worn by footsoldiers, called legionaries, were very similar.

FIGHTING WEAPONS

The helmet was only part of a soldier's equipment for battle. He also wore body armour, made of hinged metal plates or chain mail. His shield protected him, too. This consisted of thin strips of wood glued together. Felt or leather was glued onto the layered wood. The Roman soldier's main weapon was a short sword with a blade about 50 centimetres long. He also carried a dagger and spears.

The shield weighed about 6 kilograms and was decorated with metal strips and paint.

A legionary soldier's body armour. Iron plates are hinged to fit the body tightly but allowed the soldier to move and fight.

The iron sword in its decorated scabbard was carried on the soldier's right side.

Each legionary soldier carried two spears for battle. The long iron tip was fixed onto a wooden shaft.

Daggers were often decorated and were about 25 centimetres long.

Guards were posted along the walls, on the
guard towers and at the fort's four gates.

SOLDIERS OF RANK

As in any army, there were Roman soldiers
of different rank and soldiers for particular
jobs.

Legionary   Cavalryman   Standard
bearer

Centurion   Auxiliary

THE FORT

Roman forts were always laid out very
carefully by the army's engineers. Each
night, when the army was on the march, a
temporary camp was made. The soldiers
slept under leather tents.

But all over the Roman Empire, there were
stone or timber forts built for permanent
units of the army. Inside the fort, the
soldiers lived in barrack blocks. These
were long buildings divided into at least ten
pairs of rooms. In one room were the bunks
for eight men and a fireplace for cooking
their meals. The other room was for their
equipment and weapons.

No, it's not a bridge for traffic! This is the Pont du Gard aqueduct which carried water across the River Gardon to Nîmes, southern France. The water ran in a channel at the top above arches nearly 50 m high. Each day it provided 400 litres of water for each of the 50,000 people living in Nîmes. The aqueduct (the word means water carrier) was over 50 km long.

ROMAN BUILDERS

The Romans are famous for designing and building huge structures like aqueducts, roads and buildings for entertainment. The engineers' job was to work out whether the building would actually stand the strain. Surveyors were needed to measure out the plans drawn up by the architects. In most of the countries they conquered, the Romans were the first people to build in brick and in stone held together by mortar (lime and sand mixed with water).

THE GROMA

The surveyor would look over one of the arms of the *groma* and sight a straight line to someone holding a rod. Another person further away could then have his rod positioned on that straight line.

This is a surveyor's instrument, called a *groma*. It was used to mark out straight lines and was especially useful for engineers building straight roads.

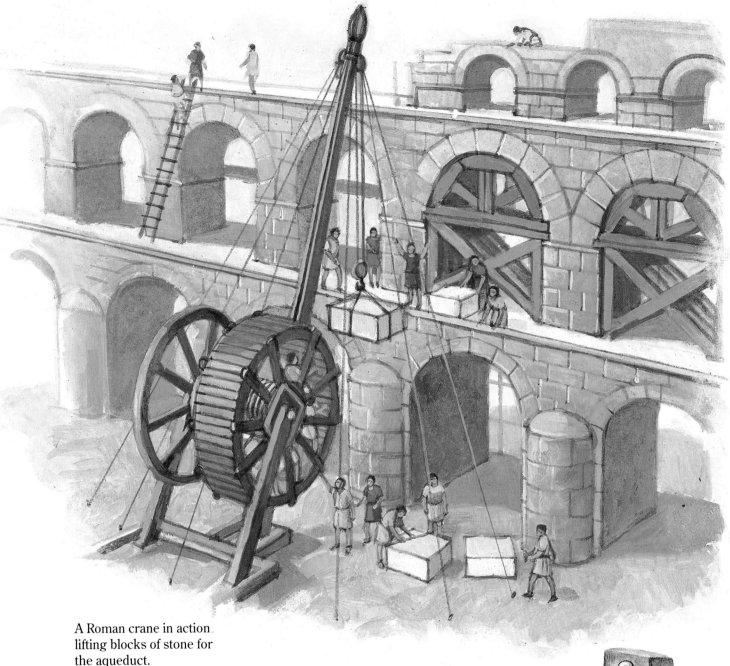

A Roman crane in action
lifting blocks of stone for
the aqueduct.

BUILDING THE AQUEDUCT

The Pont du Gard was built during the reign
of the Emperor Claudius (27 BC to AD 14).
The Roman engineers had a variety of
'machinery' to help them build. Here you
can see the great wooden device used for
lifting blocks of stone. It is 'powered' by
people working the treadmill. Skilled
workers cut the stone to the right shape for
flat blocks or for the arches. At each stage of
the aqueduct, the builders had to get the
stones level using an instrument called a
chorobates.

Many streets had fountains and water troughs filled by
water piped through underground lead pipes. From
here people could fetch the water they needed to use in
their houses and flats.

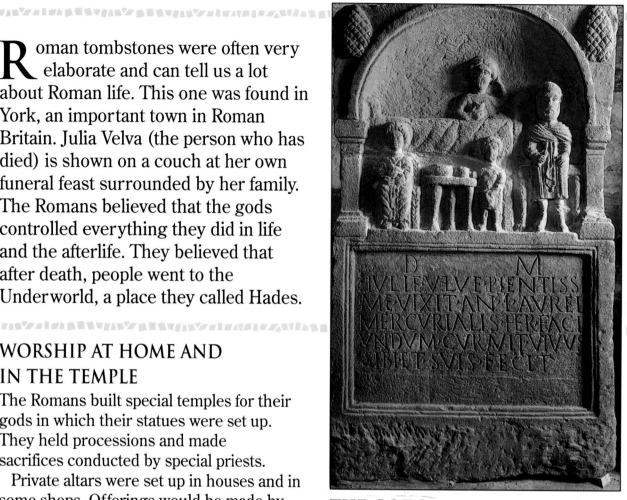

Roman tombstones were often very elaborate and can tell us a lot about Roman life. This one was found in York, an important town in Roman Britain. Julia Velva (the person who has died) is shown on a couch at her own funeral feast surrounded by her family. The Romans believed that the gods controlled everything they did in life and the afterlife. They believed that after death, people went to the Underworld, a place they called Hades.

WORSHIP AT HOME AND IN THE TEMPLE

The Romans built special temples for their gods in which their statues were set up. They held processions and made sacrifices conducted by special priests.

Private altars were set up in houses and in some shops. Offerings would be made by the father on behalf of the family to the special 'gods of the household'.

Household altar

THE GODS

For most of the period of the Roman Empire, Roman people believed in a large number of gods. They even took on gods worshipped by other peoples, such as the Greeks and the Egyptians. Some Romans continued to worship Jesus Christ after he had been crucified, even though it was against the law. Christianity did in fact become the official religion of the Empire some years later.

MINERVA was the goddess of wisdom, crafts, trades and industry. The Romans believed she invented musical instruments. She is often shown in armour because she guided fighters in battle.

Professional actors and musicians were employed to lead the funeral procession to the grave.

FUNERALS

At different times in the Roman period, people were either cremated (their bodies burnt and the ashes collected in an urn) or buried. Cemeteries were only allowed outside the town walls and were usually at the sides of the road.

The Romans believed that the dead person would go on a journey to live with the gods of the dead, called the Manes.

JUPITER was the god of the sky and king of all the gods. He was called 'the greatest and the best'. His wife, Juno, was the patron goddess of women.

APOLLO was a Greek god worshipped by the Romans. He could tell the future and the Romans made offerings to him to reveal his secrets.

MITHRAS was originally worshipped by the Persians. Soldiers and merchants began to worship him and temples were put up all over the Empire where mysterious rites were carried out.

NEPTUNE was the god of water and the sea. He is usually shown with his three-pronged spear, called a trident.

ANSWERS TO MYSTERY OBJECT BOXES

Page 8: This piece of farm equipment was the equivalent of a modern combine harvester. It was called a *vallus*. Its wide blades were pushed by a donkey or an ox into the wheat crop. They cut off the heads and gathered them in a scoop.

Page 17: This little object is a personal toilet set, including an ear-scoop and a nail-cleaner.